Love Returned

A Daughter's Journey

By Joanne Sherrod W. Sigler

Hickory Sticks 1964

B.Luby

**Greatfully Dedicated
to My wonderfully caring family, friends,
and to the memory of Mother and Daddy.**

INTRODUCTION

My purpose in writing this book is to try to help those who have the responsibility of caring for elderly parents and friends. We are fortunate to have guidance in other areas of behavior, but no one has survived to coach us on the do's and don't of how to be an old person or how it feels to be sick and dying. Take a minute – place yourself in the position of that old person as he or she explains aches, pains, pills, etc., and the inevitable act of <u>welcoming</u> or the <u>fear</u> of dying. Then, be the listener while taking notes which would be too pathetic and emotional to review – much less kept and passed on to your loved ones. When that occasion comes, the patient will attempt to be patient of what comes next and those attending will attend with kindness, respect and love. They call us "care-givers" which covers a wide collection of human beings. My husband, sister and brother-in-law fell into that category rather quickly.

Well, let me tell you right now, it is <u>strictly</u> "on job training". The transition from being "cared for" <u>to</u> "caring for" is horrendous – sometimes comical – heart-warming <u>and</u> heart-breaking! Regardless of our maturing and as long as our parents are living, deep down in their beings we are still their children, their charge, their responsibilities – until they die. As to our thinking we are still their children until the day arrives for us to be the parent and they our children. My prescription is this because our family was at this point and we learned to: 1) take one day at a time and remember each has <u>only</u> 24 hours; 2) have a family and others who support your actions and decisions 100%, no questions asked, and; 3) a gargantuan sense of humor, without which a mental breakdown is eminent!

Sometimes my <u>seven</u> years have seemed like seventy times seven, but I've learned many important and unimportant aspects of this thing called "Life". I'd like to share some of my experiences with you. We've always looked to our parents for answers, guidance and support. When we don't know the answer to something – at any age – we say, "I'll ask my Mother or Daddy". Immediately I realized that was impossible and felt so inadequate. As well as I can describe it, it's as if my family was on a Totem Pole – Daddy and Mother on top, my sister, me and then our children. All of a sudden the top of the pole is eliminated – leaving me exposed to the world. How could I answer questions – had I listened and learned? What if I couldn't measure up? Could I go back and look through their eyes? I felt like the cares of the world were on my shoulders! My family had no warning, training or preparation for this moment. So, at the ages of 88 and 83, it became apparent that now was the time, per their request, to leave their big home of 62 years and find a small apartment. They approved – and the move took place.

Flora Belle, O.P. Sherrod and the 3020 William Street white house formed a union. The three were inseparable from 1924 until the day it was sold. The original information in the newspaper stated that the purchase price was $1,875.00 for Lot L in Sunny Slope Subdivision. It had a small house of four rooms. However, during the next fifty years it was enlarged with more rooms, 2 screened porches and 2 patios. This house and yard played host to thousands of parties of every description.

We are all attached to houses we've lived in because that's what made them a home. From birth until 25 years of age, 3020 was my nest - the same room with probably 15 coats of paint on the walls and furniture rearranged in every conceivable way! It had been empty for several weeks, but I couldn't resist visiting it just one more time while it was still attached to Mother and Daddy – and me! Thank God it sold to the first person who looked at it. I don't know if I could have endured the "real estate waltz".

The day the final papers were to be signed, I awoke with knots in my stomach, throat, heart and head. What was I doing? Looking at the clock, I realized I had one hour to spare and decided to "go home" one last time. Orvis and I arranged to meet in the attorney's office which afforded me the opportunity to be by myself – thankfully. As I got out of the car I realized I still had the house key on my key chain! Upon seeing our home, and holding that key, a flood of memories of Mother and Daddy came pouring in. I'd like to take a moment and share some of those memories with you.

First of all who were these people I had lived with and loved all my life? Perhaps you will understand our connection and their influence on my life. I would like to introduce you to my parents, Flora Belle Walton Sherrod and Oscar Penic Sherrod born in 1901 and 1897 respectively. They were the best parents in the world – to me and my sister, Betty Jane, known as B.J., who was seven ½ years older than I. Having married on December 31, 1923, in Waskom, Texas, they died on October 29, 1988 and January 16, 1990 – each within a day of their birthdays. What a marriage! I never heard them argue, but if they did it was behind closed doors. A quick profile will inform you that they were ordinary middle class, completely sober (except for a very small drink on their anniversary), non-smokers (but only after Daddy was diagnosed in 1938 with tuberculosis), fun-loving while hosting many parties at their Hickory Sticks Farm, devoted parents, Christians, loyal to their families and America.

Mother's side of my personal tree was everything to me, which I only found out when it came time for me to be a mother. By my observation she was a wonderful wife, by our close association she was fair, loving, religious, supportive, fun-loving and original in everything. She didn't want anything like someone else had! This quotation I read recently scared me, "There are moments when you are your mother and your daughter at the same time." We must, as mothers, be connected to our history and gender so that we live in our children's hearts forever. Cutting that famous cord only separates us by space. We are left with a "belly button" as a daily reminder. Check it out and be thankful.

These things I remember most about Mother. She loved flowers and shared them with everyone. She was always at home at 3:00 pm except for her bridge day so Kiki stayed late and filled her place. She confided in me that the highlight of her day was when I would come in the back door from school. She said I was the "apple of her eye". She always called everyone "Dahlin". She never wore slacks until she was seventy when Daddy bought her a pantsuit. I remember the way she walked, answered the phone, whistled me home from Peggy's or the Bouttés, fussing at me before we both broke into laughter and smelling of Evening in Paris.

Mother's personality, as I finally figured out, was a combination of Edith Bunker, Scarlett O'Hara, General McArthur and Mary, mother of Jesus. Simply put – a sweet naive soul, a beautiful Southern lady, a strict disciplinarian and a deeply religious woman. There were two areas of her personality which always stood out. She could never accept a personal compliment. As we were standing in their yard in the sun she looked at me and said, "Dahlin', your hair is just shining." To which I replied, "Your hair is shining, too." Since we both had white hair, the sun reflected off it. Mother wasn't satisfied so I handed her a mirror. She studied herself with her eyes bouncing back and forth between the two of us. Finally she returned the mirror and said, "Well, mine <u>is</u> prettier than yours." If you knew Mother, you would know she would <u>never</u> have complimented herself – only others. Maybe she just needed a little self confidence that day. She got it! Mother also never hurt anyone's feelings

– of which I am aware except sometimes those feelings were on my legs – but I deserved it.

Daddy was the complete definition of a daddy, even though we realized Mother came first. Being loved just for yourself is the essence of the word. I remember sitting in his lap being hugged, playing this little horsey went to town and being dropped between his knees and laughing until I couldn't get my breath! He wanted a boy so much that he taught me everything a little girl or boy needed to know. Not the usual things like learning to ride a bicycle, but the extra things like using a hammer – always cautioning me not to choke the handle, sawing, spitting on the point of a nail so it would go in better, swinging a baseball bat and <u>hitting</u> the ball. Of all the things he taught me, I think the love of nature means more to me than the others. Not a hunter or a fisherman, he taught me the love of growing things – trees, flowers, all kinds of plants. Being in the lumber business he could always tell me the kind of tree, its root system and would make me examine the leaves. He would even make an estimate as to how many linear feet of lumber a big tree might produce. He told me one time that trees are just big umbrellas which protect us from too much sun and rain. I still like to think of them that way. I sure do miss my lessons.

The definition outside our home was that of loyalty to the K.C.S. Railway. His 46 years of being a company man made him just as proud as did his family. His two jobs in all those years dealt with the "rail bed". He personally bought every cross tie for the New Orleans to Kansas City route. When he packed his bag in the summer, I packed mine. Away we went by car to the woods where sawmills were set up temporarily to cut trees, then shape them into crossties and stack them, then they were bought with Daddy's yellow paint stamp of approval. Years later he told me that "the K.C.S. was the best railroad in the world, and I helped make it the best". Recently I found out that his great-grandfather owned the third railroad in the United States – it's no wonder that he was a company man to the end. When I hear a train whistle, I always think of Daddy.

My trips on the K.C.S. up to Kansas City were wonderful! He let me accompany the conductor as he collected tickets in the chair car, help the Pullman Porters with their beds, go into the tiny kitchen in the Dining Car for a cookie and help put the big boarding step out for the passengers to step onto the train. If that didn't take up the 10 or so hours I was allowed to sit in the Club Car at the rear of the train. Since he traveled 3, 4 or 5 days a week by train or car these days were very special to me because the train and I had his "undivided attention"!

Church and Sunday School attendance at Kings Highway Christian Church was very important to the Sherrod family. Be it rain or shine there we were sitting as a family behind Mrs. Reed, the minister's wife, on the sixth row on the Epistle side. Mother and Daddy loved children – all children and knew they loved gum. So began the ritual on every Saturday morning. They visited the TG&Y Variety Store and bought probably 25 packages of Wrigley's Spearmint Gum. Arriving at home Daddy sat down at the dining room table and opened each package and divided the pieces into two piles. He wrote his weekly check for the offering plate and placed it between the piles. Sunday morning he placed the piles into his suit coat pockets and the check into his shirt pocket. His organizational qualities were famous at our house. Between church and Sunday School the children, some adults and sometimes the preacher had their hands out for that sweet taste. Later the youth group presented him with a plaque which he cherished: "Presented to O.P. Sherrod for Doubling our Pleasure at Kings Highway Christian Church".

As I opened that familiar door I lingered on the screened porch remembering the glider and rocking chairs which had performed miracles for me while being rocked by Mother or Kiki and the floor where we sat as children while we played Monopoly, Jacks, Pick-Up Sticks,

Solitaire, Dominoes, Chinese Checkers – or nothing at all – just sitting with my friends and their imaginations, listening to the radio, remembering, or sometimes just alone with my thoughts.

Upon opening the front door I wondered how many loved ones had been welcomed to the Sherrod's hospitality. That living room held every Christmas tree for 62 years. It was decorated with every conceivable ball, string of lights, tinsel, angel and Santa imaginable. Those trees lived and died while giving us enjoyment with each Christmas. The furniture, lamps, knick-knacks, two Royal Dalton figurines, the wonderful oil painting of a Spanish ship which now hangs in my dining room were all pictured in their places - and in my mind's eye. The most important object, which I could still hear, was the big floor standing radio as we all sat or stood in silence while President Roosevelt was announcing the fate of Pearl Harbor. I thought my world had come to an end. The total recall of his voice, my parents' expressions as they remembered another World War, our Sunday guest, Mr. Riggs, and even my new dress I was wearing for the first time. Kiki came into the room and quietly announced dinner was ready – breaking the silence as well as today's silence I was enduring.

Our dining room welcomed many parties with its French doors opening onto the screened porch in pleasant weather. The memorable and familiar blessing by Daddy still rings in my heart, "Our most gracious, heavenly

Father....." As was the custom, Kiki worked a half day on Sundays. The third Sunday of the month she spent the day at her church usually wearing her "usher dress" which Mother had made for her. That third Sunday for the Sherrod's was spent at the Mirror Steak House, Worm's Hilltop House or Brocato's Spring Street Restaurant.

Most Sundays we had company. Our guests were friends and Dr. and Mrs. Reed from Kings Highway Christian Church. During the war there were many soldiers from Barksdale who attended church and accepted Mother's invitation for a home-cooked meal. Considering how much time they had, a game of badminton or croquet completed the day. The highlight came when our family delivered them to "Barksdale Field, the largest airfield in the world as it was before 1947 – 22,500 acres", which is, and always will be, in Shreveport, Louisiana.

Standing in the kitchen I could visualize our family sitting at the table having breakfast, dinner (not lunch) and supper. My - how things have changed. That table was huge – until I walked past it just now in my house! We ate on it, my sister and I did our homework on it, we mixed up white oleo margarine and made it yellow by using the little enclosed packet, and I painted it every summer. My most enjoyable act was eating my summertime dinner so slowly as I had to clean my plate after everyone had been excused. Then I got to finish eating with Kiki! It was our plan all along.

In this kitchen Mother and Kiki sealed their friendship. It was never limited to a kitchen's function, but shared almost every phase of their feelings and activities. Mother made blue uniforms for Kiki because all the other maids in the neighborhood wore white. She also made her evening dresses to go dance with her date at the Calanthean Building on Texas Avenue. Since Daddy traveled these two women shared this household from the ages of 30 and 18, respectively, and had a lot in common. Kiki had started to work for us when I was born. Oh, if those kitchen walls could talk! And, I thought I could smell those hot, homemade yeast rolls coming out of the oven!

As I passed through the hall I could still hear Mother. "Joanne or Betty Jane, if you don't get off that phone I just don't know what I'll do." Of course, with one phone, it only had a six foot cord – no privacy – every spoken word was public information. (Ed. Note – 2011 – we've come full circle.)

The back bedroom was Mother and Daddy's. The gas floor heater, when lit in the winter, took the chill off the room after a cold winter's night. There was Mother's sewing machine which produced clothes that filled my closet with anything I needed – or wanted. Between the beds was Mother's cedar chest full of memories and treasures. Words of wisdom abounded in their room. "Don't sit on my bed", "Pretty is as pretty does", "Do unto other as you would have others do unto you" – I remember them all.

The back sleeping porch always had a breeze. It had 2 double beds and canvas awnings around three sides. My favorite time on the porch was Sunday mornings in the summertime when Daddy would get in bed with me and read the funny paper regardless of my age! Then he would look up at the telephone wires full of birds and try to convince me they were having Bird Sunday School! I still believe that!

The tiny bathroom was a miracle in itself. How the four of us managed to take care of our personal needs without humiliating each other, I'll never understand. My unforgettable memory of this room was being caught riding my bicycle on Kings Highway. When I arrived at 3020 William Street, Daddy took me to the bathroom and switched me good! With hardly any room to move his hits found their targets – my legs – and it was summer! Maybe that's why I love to jitterbug – it reminds me of Daddy.

My sister Betty Jane got married when I was in the seventh grade. I finally had a room (and a closet) to myself! I even had my own radio! It was used mostly in the summer especially on rainy days while Peggy and I listened intently to those Soap Operas which played from 9:00 am until about 4:00 pm – "Young Widow Brown", "Stella Dallas", "Guiding Light", "Lorenzo Jones" – I'm sure there were others. Honestly, we didn't spend too much time in our bedrooms because we had too many things to do outside. However, one incident does stand out – the first day we got our attic fan. It was a cool night as I prepared for bed that night in July. I opened my windows, put on my shortie pj's, threw back the bedspread and sheet, jumped into bed and got in a spread eagle position. With the forced breeze blowing across me I knew I must be the coolest person in town. As a result I got the worst summer cold I've ever had! How much I was to learn about heating and cooling later in life.

I opened the back door and looked at the big yard where in the summer we played badminton, croquet, climbed a huge Oak tree, camped out overnight, etc, etc, etc! Mother had her beautiful rose beds and Daddy had his blackberry vines. But the best thing was the swing – which knew no age. The frame was of 6″ x 6″ creosote posts 20' high with a swing that took you up, up and away. Then I'd hear Mother say, "Oh, how I'd love to go up in a swing, up in the air so high". While I was there I sat down to swing and recited the verse. I could feel

Daddy's push every time I went back - "higher, Daddy, higher!" From the back porch Mother would say, "That's high enough" – always the cautious one.

THAT was my 3020 William Street in Sunny Slope Subdivision, Shreveport, Louisiana. The land had once been owned by the Fullilove family whose wonderful two-story antebellum home stood on the corner of Samford Street and Jackson Street (now Glen Oak). These two streets and my William Street were named for their sons.

The time had finally come – my hour of sharing and remembering, which I still treasure, had come to an end. I closed and locked the front door and removed that front door key which had been on my keychain seemingly forever.

I left crying, of course, but felt like I had temporarily turned the clock back to how I wanted to remember my white house. Today I'm so full of thankfulness for all those moments. I arrived at the attorney's office to find my husband waiting to take charge of me so that I could function somewhat normally. Every time they pointed to a line for me to sign my name, I signed and cried, behind my dark glasses of course. I really felt I had betrayed my parents by doing this nasty deed – but as the saying goes, "someone has to do it". The next day I felt like I had reached another plateau of this tremendous task. After a few days I recovered, to a point, and tried to be ready for the next painful experience. Was it never to end?

As I explained before, my family was quite innocent in recognizing the fact that Mother and Daddy, at 83 and 88, had begun to have problems. Still active in their daily lives probably reassured us they would be the exception of/to the "old age and failing" category. My Mother? My Daddy? NO! My sister and family lived in Houston, Texas, and kept in touch by phone with them. I probably visited "for a minute" to check on them 3 or 4 times a week. Anne and Liz visited also, as did the Sherrod's friends.

One day on my checking in schedule to my amazement Mother explained their "problem". "We need to move out of this neighborhood and find an apartment." We 3 talked calmly about this, and I came home to Orvis as a nervous wreck! There is a book to teach us "how to do" every function of life. However, we've had no training on how to be the center of a role reversal – that of taking over and making decisions for one's parents – which I feel goes against what I've been programmed to do. My parents always knew what was best for me, and that was that, no questions asked. I lived at home for my first 25 years until marriage, hence a rather sheltered life. For the next nineteen years through marriage, 2 children, widowed, remarriage – they were always my most treasured supporters. One can't imagine how I felt when I had to make monumental decisions about my parents' daily lives.

Finding an apartment suitable for them seemed an impossible task. However, Fairfield Oaks was in a close, familiar area so our work was cut out for us. I called my sister and made plans. The move, which included furniture, etc, choices made from closets filled for 62 years were completed in just one day. They seemed to feel comfortable surrounded by their possessions, but after 62 years it just wasn't the same. Mother seemed to adjust but Daddy was completely disoriented. They would leave in the car and upon returning could not seem to find their apartment. It was sad and, yes, pitiful and within 2 weeks Daddy became ill and had to be hospitalized. Then Mother became ill and she, too, was hospitalized. They were on different floors of the same hospital. At this point, and after painful deliberation, my husband, my sister, her husband and I reached the obvious conclusion. A nursing home was the only answer.

A novice might approach this quest as one might knock on the door of a Holiday Inn on a stormy vacation night – "Hello, got any vacancies?" Well, this is definitely not the way it is in reality! My husband began "making rounds". "Yes, we have a couple who doesn't want to be separated." "Well, Mr. Smith will probably be dying within the week so we could take your Daddy but not your Mother." "Yes, they will pay cash each month. Yes, they are on medication. No, they are not physically or mentally handicapped." Plus a thousand more questions! Indeed, this was not the Holiday Inn. <u>Their</u> lodgers weren't asked these questions, and 100% of them left of their own accord. After a week's labor of screening, my husband decided on three homes for my sister and me to make the final decision. Within 2 days the choice was made. Our parents were placed in their new home, and we felt somewhat satisfied.

With my deep feelings of guilt, I tried to rationalize the move. From being self-sufficient, we thought, to being completely incapable of caring for themselves – this obviously was the next step. Hard? You bet it was – for everyone, but it had to be done. Several days later I wrote the following letter

Dear Mother and Daddy,

This is a very difficult letter to write; however, I will try my best to express my thoughts. You both have been excellent examples of parents for me to pattern my life as a parent. Being your daughter for almost 53 years has been a very happy experience, and I think I've made you proud of me. You've taken good care of me all my life even though I've been married. You've always had my best interests at heart. Now it is my turn to take care of you.

Look around you at this nice retirement home. This is your new home – a place to live together. These good people will take good care of you. All you have to do is sleep, eat and enjoy the other people.

Daddy, you've always loved to visit. Everyone here has lived through the same times you have – walking 5 miles to school, working on a farm, serving in the First World War, the Depression, having children and a good job. You have so many things to share with other people. I've never known you to be without conversation.

Mother, just think – you don't have to cook, clean house, wash dishes, or anything you've done for 62 years of housekeeping. Now all you have to do is eat, sleep and enjoy the other people. You can brag on your children and grandchildren, talk about sewing, flowers, recipes, parties and your church. Sharing with others is a privilege. Then there is the time you need to be by yourself – to read, watch TV, write letters to your family telling about your younger years that you probably haven't even told us yet.

I know that you still think you two can live in your own home and take care of each other, but when you lived in the apartment we found out that was impossible. Now we've found you this nice, clean, safe and pleasant place to live together. It might be a little hard to adjust at first, but after a while, if you try, you'll love it. We'll come to visit you as often as possible, bring you to our house for Sunday dinner and take you for rides. Please try very, very hard to understand that I'm trying to take care of you the best way I know how – just like you took such good care of me. I love you both with all my heart.
Joanne

One phase of this process is that someone has to take charge of all the bills: the nursing home bills, the doctor bills, the pharmacy bills, the insurance forms, Medicare records, the checkbook, broken eyeglasses, hearing aid batteries, deodorant, toothpaste, soap. Endless – endless records to be kept. It goes on and on and on! This all fell into my husband's hands – for all these years!

One day, after my husband had spent hours at the desk, he looked at me and said, "Your dad is 88, your mother is 83 – Jo, you will never die." I thought, dear God, is this what my sons-in-law will be saying about me some day? This was a bottomless pit which neither of us really minded. It's sorta like an unexpected pregnancy. You did it, you accepted it, loved it and lived with it and hoped that the first grade would be sooner than it was!

Losing grandparents to death is final, but losing them to a nursing home is even harder. They are there, but can't participate in all the fun things. Although my own grandparents died when I was very young, I have enjoyed seeing my children with my parents. The bond between them is so full of sweet memories. Hopefully, I can learn by example to "grandmother" perfectly. The following is a letter written by my daughter Liz. Through her words one can understand that special relationship between my parents and their grandchildren.

Dear Mamma and Daddié,

I sure do miss seeing you both since you went to the nursing home. I hope you never forget how much I love you both and how much you mean to me. I will never, never forget the two of you and all the memories we have shared. The two of you are the best grandparents a girl could ever have.

Thank you for being so good to me. I remember all the cokes we drank when my friends and I stopped by your house on our 20 mile "Walk for Fun". Who else's grandparents would have had 30 cold cokes ready to drink? Thank you for the peanut butter sandwiches you made when you took Anne and me to Texarkana on the K.C.S. Railroad. Thank you for the chocolate chip cookies you mailed to me in college, the money you sent to me in Puerto Rico so I could buy the shoes I wanted, for letting me drive Daddié's truck endless times up and down the driveway when I was just 6 years old. We waved to you, Mamma, every time we passed the kitchen window, surely we drove you crazy. Thank you for buying malted milk balls at Sears. Thank you for going in halves with me when I didn't have enough money to buy something I "needed". Thank you for making good hamburgers and spaghettios and for not telling Mom when we were bad. Thank you for talking to me about the Depression and helping me to open my eyes to the past – I made an A+ on my interview. Thank you for making the cross stitch sampler I sewed to come true. "If Mother says no – ask Grandmother. If all else fails, ask Grandfather." Thank you for teaching me the true meaning of being a good grandparent. Thank you for giving me things to talk about, "When I was little my Grandparents and I used to .....". Thank you Daddié for teaching me how to be car sick by constantly pumping the gas pedal. Thank you for teaching me how to make the best toast with strawberry preserves. Thank you for waking me up in the middle of the night to go to the bathroom! Thank you for taking the place of my own Daddy for 2 ½ years. Thank you for all the gum....and cavities! Thank you for teaching me how to cane pole fish. Thank you for teaching me to say Grandmother, thee, thee, thee when my 2 front teeth weren't there. Thank you for pinching me on my bottom and making that funny noise. Thank you for letting me put shaving cream on my face and shave with an empty razor while you were really shaving. Thank you for letting me ride on your back, for swinging me higher than <u>any girl has ever swung before</u>. Thank you for all the times I got to sit on your lap and be loved. Thank you for building our playhouse in the country, for giving me presents, too, when it was Anne's birthday. Thank you for letting us spend the night at your house, and teaching me to like the Lawrence Welk Show. Thank you for telling me soooo many times the stories of <u>*The Three Bears*</u> and <u>*Red Riding Hood and The Big Bad Wolf*</u>. Thank you for building my bug box out of the Hush Puppy shoe box, which I still have. Thank you for picking those berries so we could have all those cobblers. Thank you for raising your daughter right so she could, in turn, raise her daughters to be good little girls and proper ladies. Thank you for always looking so nice when you left your house. Thank you for being loved by so many people. Thank you for letting me start out sleeping with Mamma and then picking me up and letting me spend the rest of the night with you. And – again – thank you, thank you, thank you for saying, "You'll never know how much I love you", "I love you more than I do anyone else, you are my favorite", which I am sure you told all your other grandchildren! Let me just say these things all back to you because I <u>do</u> love you more than anyone else, you <u>are</u> my favorite and I <u>do</u> know how much you love me! I'll never forget those wet kisses, too.

I'd better go because I'm running out of tears. I love you both so much, my darlings.

Your favorite,
Liz

When I read Liz's letter I began to understand that I was not ALONE in my loss of Mother and Daddy. I'm sure their "Grand" connection spoke for Anne and her cousins Johnny, Janey and Julie.

The following weeks were probably the worst of my life. I felt helpless and hopeless as I looked at the clean slate in front of me. I was waiting for the next chapters of my life to begin without the support of my parents through NO fault of their own. Please God, put me on the top of your list for guidance and direct me in every phase of my life!

There is nothing like experience! When Mother told me that experience was the best teacher, she really knew what she was talking about. Taking that first plane ride, eating your first bite of homemade ice cream, having your first child – all of them were new. And how <u>do</u> you know what being a parent is until you've had children? How do you know what heartache is until your parents go into a nursing home? You have to experience it. All of a sudden I tried to remember all the things my friends had told me about their parents in a nursing home. Well – <u>my</u> parents would be different – HELP!

At this point I was in bad shape, and it had only been three months! I tried to see my parents every day, and then I would cry all the way home. I would wake up during the night and wonder if they were cold – or hot – or even hungry. I was really back to Baby Care 101, and with the same worries. Every time the phone rang I was afraid it concerned them. I never felt comfortable leaving town. I felt trapped, guilty, angry, depressed and miserable. I felt the burden was on me completely. I just began to wonder – do all the children and caregivers feel as I do?

I met a friend at a party and began sharing my feelings about my parents, whom she knew. She had gone through a similar experience so she listened with a sympathetic heart. Several days later she called informing me that I had an appointment with Dr. Pugh, her Senior Minister. I was a little hesitant, but agreed to go. I kept that appointment, and Dr. Pugh literally saved my life. He had cared for his parents until their deaths, so I knew his words were coming from hands-on experience. The common sense and spiritual help he offered have been my guidelines and proven to be my salvation in coping. He offered support, understanding and helped me to accept my job. With his encouragement I looked "inside" for solutions. My attitude had to be addressed. I had to get a grip on my own feelings before I could handle Mother and Daddy's feelings. I felt complete frustration, and realized I had to face head-on my new problem – making decisions for myself. To come to my own conclusions was going to be best for me. Acting on my decisions afforded me to take responsibility for myself. I was forced to utter aloud that which I was keeping inside. Then I began to listen to my feelings. His advice was this. I must accept my position and do the best I could. There was no need to be upset by other people's actions. Make decisions with the help of those who love you and your parents. Try not to think you are alone – there's always spiritual help and professional help and don't be ashamed to ask. It's all right to be angry because you have no control. The choice is yours to solve calmly. Communication and expressing concerns open your heart. It is the only true peace from within. At the end of our meeting he asked if I had been hugged that day? Since

"No" was my answer, this 80 year old minister grabbed me, hugged me and held on while I cried my heart out. This is the one time I was sure that God gave us the opportunity to let our hearts run over with tears. As I've said, this wonderful, compassionate and caring man saved my life. It only took one visit, but every time I saw him visiting the nursing home or I drove by his church, I felt a reminder of his advice surging through my heart.

Getting help is the most intelligent thing I ever did. I have reflected on it many times and have suggested it to my friends who have been in this situation. We need each other's encouragement and support in trying times like these. The caregiver's mental health has to be addressed in order to function outside as a wife, mother, grandmother, daughter, civic volunteer, friend and just plain old ME. Wearing all those hats can become a burden, because there are not enough hours in the day to fill all positions faithfully. My parents' doctor told me that I could be a wife and mother or I could be a daughter. What a choice – why couldn't I be both? Thank God I made that choice. My husband and daughters have been willing to share me with my parents in the nursing home. They have been my strength, and I thank God for them from the bottom of my heart.

Soon after Mother and Daddy were ensconced into their "Retirement Home", (I promised I would never put them into a "Nursing Home".) I received a call asking to meet with the Director. As we drove up, we saw Daddy walking down the street as fast as he could. My husband stopped the car, and I ran to meet him. I asked where he was going and he said, "Home". I finally convinced him that we should go back and find Mother. When we arrived she was saying to the nurse at the nursing station, "Dahlin', my husband and I are going to have to check out of this hotel because the accommodations aren't as nice as what we're used to. My husband has gone for a cab." There she was – the lady always – all dressed up, hat on her head, white gloves, bags packed on the floor beside her. She had that precious smile on her face hoping that the "poor accommodations" didn't hurt the "room clerk's" feelings. This had not been their first attempt to check out. The Director asked me to take their bags to my house. Mother and Daddy were so used to traveling that reaching the end of the line had not occurred to them. The time had come.

This was not the first time Daddy had tried to "go home". The police found him in Cedar Grove probably headed up Southern Avenue for Kings Highway and William Street. Thankfully he was brought back after being recognized as a nursing home resident. He had no identification, no money, no identifying marks on his body! Now they have locked doors – thank God!

Mother called me six times in one afternoon at my place of business. "Come get me and please take me home," she said. So after work I went to the nursing home to see her. I stormed into her room and wheeled her outside so that no one could hear me and proceeded to really fuss at her for bothering me at work. I told her that she would have to behave and not call me, I was busy and couldn't talk to her six times in one afternoon. She looked up at me and said, "I'm so sorry I've disappointed you, MOTHER!" Talk about "role reversal"! It was as if I had been slapped in the face – which I had experienced only once for sticking my tongue out at her. Now I can't remember which hurt more. When I got home I told my husband how I had fussed at Mother. He told me it probably didn't faze her. But I told him – it sure made me feel good! I just had to last out at the way things were. That's the only retaliation I had against a situation over which I had no control.

Daddy was moved to another nursing home while Mother stayed there. The residents there were mostly black as were the aides. Nursing homes just cannot hire enough aides to take expert care of our parents as we would prefer. There was a black aide named Betty who took a special interest in him. She pampered him, teased with him and respected this 90 year old southern gentleman. Daddy had many black men who worked for him in the lumber business for 46 years. He ordered and they obeyed – always with respect for each other. One day I caught Daddy holding Betty's hand while walking down the hall. He introduced me to her and when she left Daddy said, "You know, I don't see color any more." He had rediscovered that all it took was a mutual respect working for the same goal.

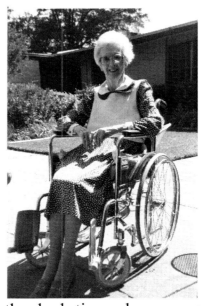

I won't relate the bad times because some were too painful, but this was painful for ME. One day after Mother had broken her hip at the nursing home, a new aide took her out of her wheelchair and sat her in her chair from home – just for a treat. The aide left and, forgetting she couldn't walk, Mother got up, fell and broke her other hip. It was a careless mistake but these things happen – quite often. While she was still confined to her bed, I came to visit and the room smelled horrible, obviously from a dirty diaper. I rang 4 times for an aide, but no one came. So guess who changed my Mother's diaper, me! Mother's diaper – what a horrible thought – my Mother wearing diapers! Can you possibly understand the total degradation of this act? So the process began. As the change progressed we talked about the weather, my husband, my children – completely ignoring the real challenge at hand. All of a sudden Mother looked at me, with that wonderful twinkle in her eye, and said, "Wonder where that awful odor is coming from?" We both died laughing. There's still just two kinds of bottoms!

We tried to take Mother and Daddy out for rides and to our home for Sunday dinners. Then it dawned on me that there were quite a few there who were mobile like Mother and Daddy. Some didn't have family on the outside and never went out. How horrible! I could not put myself in that position so I began to solve this problem.

It is no secret to my family and friends that I hate to cook. Not entirely, just the day to day stuff. If I had my way, our house would not even have a kitchen – just a nice oversized closet with a very heavy door which would not be opened too frequently. However, I do love to entertain – dinner parties, luncheons, the fancy stuff. Kiki pointed out that I was like my Mother in that respect. So I decided to have small parties for the mobile residents at the nursing home. We had a back-to-school luncheon where everyone's lunch was in a sack, an English tea party served from a silver service, a Halloween party and then a birthday party for Mother. We had 14 ladies and 2 gentlemen. After a tiny glass of wine we adjourned to the dining room. You should have heard the comments – "Oh, to be in a real 'home' again." "We're eating with real silver." "Isn't this a beautiful linen napkin – I hate paper napkins." What fun these people were having.

As we were sitting down, Daddy <u>automatically</u> went to the head of the table. I <u>automatically</u> asked him to say the blessing. Of course, his mind hadn't been "right" for a long time so I didn't know what to expect. How wonderfully surprised I was when out of his mouth came the ever so familiar – "Our gracious, heavenly Father". I cannot express what a comfortable feeling I had at that moment. I knew God had heard every word and recorded it.

Daddy was always friendly and outgoing and being a resident in a nursing home never changed him. When I arrived for my weekly visit I could always find Daddy sitting in the hall visiting with the aides or other residents. This time he was no where to be found. After asking several people, Nudie, the aide pointed inside his room. I looked in and there he sat in his wheelchair in front of the mirror just talking away. Being such a people-person, he seemed to be having a ball, especially since he had found another man, which were few and far between at the home. As I walked in he invited me to sit next to him. Then he looked back at the mirror and commented, "Now there are four of us – we can have a party." What an optimist.

Mirror, mirror on the wall, who's the fairest of them all – my Daddy!

When someone mentions nursing home to me <u>19</u> years after the fact the first word I think of is <u>frustration</u> – in every way and for all of those concerned. The dirty diaper wasn't serious but there are many other issues which need to be addressed quickly. The homes are understaffed, favoritism, competition – you name it and no nursing home escapes these problems!

I learned to surprise the nursing home staff by going to see Daddy at odd times on different days. You have to do this – just to keep them on their toes. Well, one day I found him just plain dirty, smelly and in dirty clothes. He would have been humiliated. What a dresser he had been – always a suit and tie, white starched shirt, hat – to the hilt. I checked him out and wondered what I was going to do. I finally decided, and told him we were going home to take a bath. He looked at me sort of crazy, so I laughed. I figured at 53 and 88 we could do this without too much embarrassment. I discovered he had cradle cap in his hair, his ears were filled with wax, his nose was full, and his false teeth needed to be brushed. Well – I've never seen a child enjoy a bath more! I scrubbed his back. It was like playing a game. It was just the thing to do at that time. This man, always so meticulous in his dress and personal appearance, just had to be feeling good. I washed and dried his clothes, and as he got out of the car at the nursing home, I noticed he walked just a little bit taller and straighter. After all – cleanliness is next to Godliness.

As far back as I can remember my Daddy had told me, "I don't know how I can love you any more than I love you right this minute." Today, even with his confused mind, he tells me the very same thing every Thursday. Mind you, he hasn't called me by name in well over six years, or even remembers that I'm his daughter. I think he knows that I'm someone he is attached to for some reason. I was exasperated one day and yearned to hear him say my name. Finally I said, "I'm Joanne." He looked up at me from his wheelchair and smiling said, "I used to have one of those." At last he remembered me – I think!

Minds seem to be a little cloudy at times for people in the nursing homes. Conversations are not always rewarding – sometimes entertaining. Some expressions are so embedded in our minds that we can't help but use them constantly. Mother had always called me and everyone else "Dahlin'". I think she couldn't remember names. When she would call me to come home she would start at the top of the list of loved ones, as all mothers do, and finally reach mine. I would tease her so she just started calling everyone "Dahlin'". One day I decided to take her in her wheelchair from the nursing home to the fast food restaurant next door. The day was beautiful, sun was shining and she seemed bright. We ordered and began to eat. We laughed and seemed to be having such a good time when Mother said, "Dahlin', we're having so much fun, I sure wish Joanne was with us." My heart sank. It was the first time I realized that what I saw on the outside was not necessarily what I knew had been on the inside.

Then Mother had to be moved to a second nursing home. It had to do with someone stealing her shoes during her hip surgery, her new watch (which was taken during her nap) and personal hygiene items. This happens. The second home was found and the trip began. Mother was very obliging. I had done a pretty good brain-washing job on her. Me – I was a wreck! It was like putting Anne in the first grade! The Director and aides were wonderful, accepting, loving and quite professional. I can honestly say that six years later they are the same people with the same attitudes.

As I was preparing to leave, a small 5 foot black aide realized that I was having a horrible, horrible time. I was crying my heart out. She approached me and held on to my arms and said, "Now honey, I want you to go on home and mind <u>your</u> business, and I'm going to mind your <u>Mother's</u> business." I looked down at her and emotionally put my Mother's welfare in her hands. I knew in my heart her shoulders were bigger and broader than mine. I felt she could help me carry my load until I was more in charge of myself.

After 1 ½ years of running back and forth between two nursing homes, we were finally able to have Mother and Daddy in the same room. If you don't understand what I'm saying – Mother's female roommate died, so Daddy was able to move in. There's always a waiting list for the better homes, which in this case was worth waiting for.

We thought we had prepared each of them for the reunion. Mother seemed thrilled, and we thought Daddy understood. When we picked Daddy up we told him he was going to be living with Mother for the rest of their lives. Daddy, upon seeing Mother for the first time in about six months, smiled ear to ear. However, Mother upon hearing that Daddy was to stay there said, "Well, now I'm going to have to start cooking three meals a day." I told Mother she didn't cook in the nursing home. Her response was, "That's what you think!" I started thinking, we really do relate men to cooking – all our lives!

One day as I walked into the nursing home, the nurses were laughing and looking at a picture. They shared it with me. It was a picture of my Daddy in a red nightgown. The nurse told me she had looked up several nights before and saw Daddy walking down the hall naked as a jaybird. He turned into the room of a young woman who was a quadriplegic. When this nurse arrived in the room, Daddy had opened a drawer and was putting on a nightgown – red, naturally, because it was his favorite color. The young woman in the bed was watching Daddy as he turned around. Seeing that her covers had slipped down, he carefully pulled the covers up, tucked them around her shoulders and lovingly kissed her on the forehead. It was completely natural to be tucking girls into bed having had two daughters and four granddaughters. What else would a grandfather do?

Comments overheard at a luncheon I attended one day:

1. Come get me and take me home.
2. Please change my diaper.
3. He wouldn't eat his dinner.
4. She hit the person next to her at the table.
5. He's talking ugly again.
6. They just walked out of the building and we had to find them.
7. She'll have to eat alone – she's stealing her neighbor's food.

No – it's not our children. It's years later. This was a report of our parents' actions at the nursing home. Talk about "full circle". Remember the old saying, "Twice a child, once an adult".

One wonderful aspect of this seven year experience was that my parents never complained about their "retirement home". However Mother never failed in asking, "When are you going to take us home?" My every visit answer was, "As soon as you both can get out of your wheelchairs and cook breakfast together." It seemed to satisfy them and something of which to look forward.

MOTHER'S DEATH

On October 26, 1990, I celebrated Mother's birthday by baking cookies for the most loving aides in any nursing home. Mother had recently spent several days in the hospital with congestive heart failure and had returned to the nursing home to die. Two nights before, my husband and I had been called to the home because she was very, very low. She rallied and was doing somewhat better. As I walked into her room I found her in a slight coma. All my life I've teased Mother, for which I will probably be punished by God when I die. Mother woke at the sound of my voice so I decided one more tease wouldn't hurt. "Mother, I want you to know how embarrassed and ashamed I am today. I just feel awful." With her eyes still closed she frowned, obviously questioning my feelings. After a few more barbs I revealed that the reason for my mood was due to "Today is your 89th birthday and I've never had an old woman for a mother." With closed eyes she smiled and winked her left eye. I knew my Mother was <u>still</u> in that pitiful shell of a body and <u>still</u> had her sense of humor and loved having me feel embarrassed – as if indeed I was! I left soon after, knowing that I had teased her into staying here a little longer – just for me! Selfish? You bet – but aren't our mothers there just for us – to love, to kiss, to worry, to confuse and to honor? Our cords are cut from their bodies, but that connection is life-long. My "belly-button" is a daily reminder that I did not arrive on this earth by myself – but through the love of my Daddy and Mother. Thank goodness I've always known that I was loved with all their hearts. Mother told me, "If you love me like I love you, no knife could cut our love in two." Daddy told me, "I don't know how I could love you any more than I do right this very minute."

That night I slept alone. Orvis was out of town so I went to my sewing room, furnished with my childhood furniture. As I snuggled down I felt cradled in love and fond memories, satisfied that I have been the best daughter possible, yet completely unable to change the obvious end which was fast approaching. I fell asleep remembering a million sweet reflections of being a daughter to the best mother anyone could ever have had.

The next morning when I awoke I called the nursing home to check on Mother – no change. I told the nurse I was to have an early lunch with friends and would be there by 12:30. She said not to hurry, that sometimes these things take several days. During lunch, my friends, whom I have known for 45 years, and I commented on how important friendship is, especially "old" friends who have shared troubles and treasures. Upon finishing lunch, I looked up to see my daughters coming into the restaurant. My happiness to see them made me unaware of their mission – Mother had passed away. I cried, but it was a cry of relief. Mother was ready and I was ready, but realization is still hard to take.

We are only humans, but especially are we still daughters. The last thing Nudie, her favorite sitter heard from my Mother's lips was – "I'm going, Joanne." She always shared her happiness with me, and this was the biggest trip she had ever taken and wanted me to know that her train was leaving the station on its way to Paradise. She had waited patiently for 89 years and one day. Mother died of natural causes.

At Mother's funeral the minister read a poem which was found in her Bible. She put it there I'm sure when <u>her</u> mother died, but I find consolation now.

"When God claimed my mother – my heart's love;
And took her home to dwell with Him above;
I ne'er have felt he loosed the tie
That bound her heart to mine on earth, so I
Find comfort in the thought that she must be
A guardian angel keeping watch o'er me."

Since Mother died, I'm reminded by friends how lucky I was to have had her as long as I did. I remember how sorry I felt for those friends whose mothers died at early ages. Now they say that they are the fortunate ones, because they escaped the trauma of old age, long illnesses, loss of memory and recognition, the nursing home experience and the same question – "When am I going back home?"

Now I'm glad Mother went first. Men can always take care of themselves – or so we've been told. I would have felt even more responsible, because Mother would have been so vulnerable without Daddy. After 67 years of marriage, what can you expect? Now Daddy is not even aware of Mother's death, and that's okay. It would break his heart. Yesterday, for the first time in almost 7 years, he asked me when I was coming back. I told him I'd be back next Thursday. Lord, I hope he doesn't realize it will be seven days! At times I have a guilty conscience, but I've had to play "tough love" in order to survive. Learning to let go – a little at a time.

<u>DADDY'S DEATH</u>

When the phone rang at 7:15 a.m., I knew it was bad news. "Your Dad got choked on his breakfast, and we tried CPR. Now we've called 911. They'll be taking him to the hospital soon." We got dressed quickly and found Daddy in the emergency room. When I was allowed to go in, there was Daddy with the EKG strapped to his chest and an oxygen mask – lying very still. Those attending him were quietly going about their chores. The Emergency Room doctor took us to a little room "to wait". Then I decided I needed to see Daddy. When I went in he looked so still and quiet. His pulse was still beating – very slowly. I stroked his little bald head and kissed him three times. It was the last seal of an "X" as he used to sign my birthday cards. I returned to the waiting room and shortly the doctor arrived with the inevitable report. Daddy died at 7:45 a.m. I cried. Orvis cried. The end had come. All of a sudden I had an empty feeling – an aloneness. I loved him so much. I enjoyed him as a buddy, admired him as a friend and adored him as a father. I can still feel his arm around my shoulders patting me, still feel the moisture on my forehead when he kissed me 3 times – always 3 times – and the way he held my cheek and told me, "I don't know how I could love you any more than I do right this minute." I was my Daddy's baby and always will be – knowing that he loved me with all his heart. I found this in his own handwriting in his wallet. "Love is something that lasts for a full lifetime. This truly is the thing that keeps families together." I'll treasure his memory as long as I live. He wasn't perfect, but he was my Daddy.

Daddy died on January 14, 1992. As our family gathered at our house before Daddy's funeral, B.J. and I realized that our children had disappeared, but decided they wanted to be together. As we were ushered to our seating area the first thing we saw were Wrigley Spearmint gum pieces placed on the pews. Our old and dear friend Charles Ravenna spoke and explained the situation, "Yes, please chew your gum." When we met with the minister I told him I wanted his funeral to be a birthday party – and what a party! He exposed all of Daddy's wonderful qualities of resourcefulness, devoted employee, church man, compassionate neighbor, loving husband, father and grandfather, lover of life. A man who loved and was loved for almost 95 years. As the minister said, "Today, January 16th, is O. P.'s birthday party, really a double party. Today we celebrate his birth and long life, but also we celebrate his rebirth and eternal life – coming and going on the same day. Actually it is more correctly said of this railroad man – arrival, departure, arrival – from one station to another. From the delights of earth to the even more awesome delights of Heaven. When the tears of sadness flow, let them water this family's spirits and bring forth laughter and delight in one who touched their lives so deeply. May Mr. Sherrod's ideals and principles continue to mold and shape the values of those he loved."

As the pall bearers were placing their boutonnières on his casket at Forest Park Cemetery a K.C.S. train, heading south, blew its whistle and those present laughed and clapped! It was a proper farewell!

IT'S OVER

It was almost seven years to the day of commitment of caring for two very important people in my life, who dedicated their lives to giving and helping others. Filling the role of care-giver is just what it says – giving care and with that commitment comes a lot of lessons to be learned. At first I didn't mind, I rather enjoyed it. Our children had gone to college or married, the dogs had died, and it was just the two of us doing whatever we wanted to do. We traveled and turned our backs on Shreveport with no responsibilities. All of a sudden it happened – no warning. With my sister living out of town, the day to day problems sometimes became monumental. So we did the best we could – every day – every night. I used to worry about the late night phone calls coming from our children – now the calls came from the nursing home – 24 hours a day, seven days a week. Mother and Daddy were my sole responsibility and sometimes I resented it. I was fortunate that I could talk to the head nurse about this. She advised me to stop coming so often – back off – take time for myself. After all, they didn't know Wednesday from Sunday. It just hurt so that their minds weren't as they should be and considering my personality, I could not believe that I couldn't "fix" them. I expected too much of myself and others and that confused me even more. I had to teach myself that this was the way things were going to be whether I liked it or not – or as Mother used to say, "like it or lump it". The choice was there. Even if they didn't know me, I sure knew them and couldn't turn my back on them. A friend wrote to me recently that we remain children until our parents die and after their deaths we begin to mature. I guess in those seven years my parents were dying a little bit every day, and I was maturing a little bit every day. In a word I was learning to "let go", which is essential to any loving relationship – but, oh, how hard it is! As I've said, without my husband, children, and friends I would not have survived on a day to day basis. My visits went from three days a week – to two days a week – to only on Thursdays. My God! Letting go of a <u>lifelong</u> relationship is hard, but I had to. I know in my heart that I have done everything humanly possible for my parents' well-being, comfort and joy since 1985. I have no regrets, only a feeling of content and peace. My task is over. I did the best I could. Being a care-giver makes you look back and wonder if I passed the test, did I do good, did I make the right decisions? There's so much second-guessing, but I know in my heart that I did unto them as they had already done unto me. Most importantly was the fact that they trusted me completely with their lives. I was just "returning their love".

Epilogue

As a widow at 34 I promised myself that I would do all I could to help my friends when they were left alone. I fulfilled my promise. Now that I have survived the care and death of my parents, I have promised myself that I will try to help others in this situation. I hope that through this close introspection of my feelings over the years, that I can trust my daughters and their husbands to use the same loving care and make the best decisions for me when the time comes for me to make "the big move". I don't want them to feel any of the trauma I experienced. I've left them this collection of instructions to follow.

Hopefully, they'll use my guidelines to fulfill their obligation of caring for their aged parent – if I should live that long.

Thank goodness God made us all different. Therefore there are no set rules as to how we should react to every situation. We do the best we can while gaining knowledge and guidance from our own experiences and those of others. Remember: 1. Take one day at a time; 2. Ask for support; 3. Find and keep a good sense of humor; 4. Write your own story.

Joanne Sherrod Whittington Sigler